For Danny and Kevin
–P.M.

For Juana and Sally, and Robert and Don
–L.E.

Dial Books for Young Readers
An imprint of Penguin Random House LLC, New York

Text copyright © 2020 by Peter Mercurio
Illustrations copyright © 2020 by Leo Espinosa

Penguin supports copyright. Copyright fuels creativity, encourages diverse
voices, promotes free speech, and creates a vibrant culture. Thank you for
buying an authorized edition of this book and for complying with copyright
laws by not reproducing, scanning, or distributing any part of it in any form
without permission. You are supporting writers and allowing Penguin to con-
tinue to publish books for every reader.

Dial & colophon is a registered trademark of Penguin Random House LLC.

Visit us online at penguinrandomhouse.com

Library of Congress Cataloging-in-Publication Data is available.

Printed in China
ISBN 9780525427544

10 9 8 7 6 5 4 3 2 1

Design by Jasmin Rubero
Text set in Avenir

The art for this book was created digitally with Photoshop and mixed media.

OUR SUBWAY BABY

Peter Mercurio

illustrated by **Leo Espinosa**

Dial Books for Young Readers

Some babies are born into their families. Some are adopted. This is the story of how one baby found his family in the New York City subway.

Exit

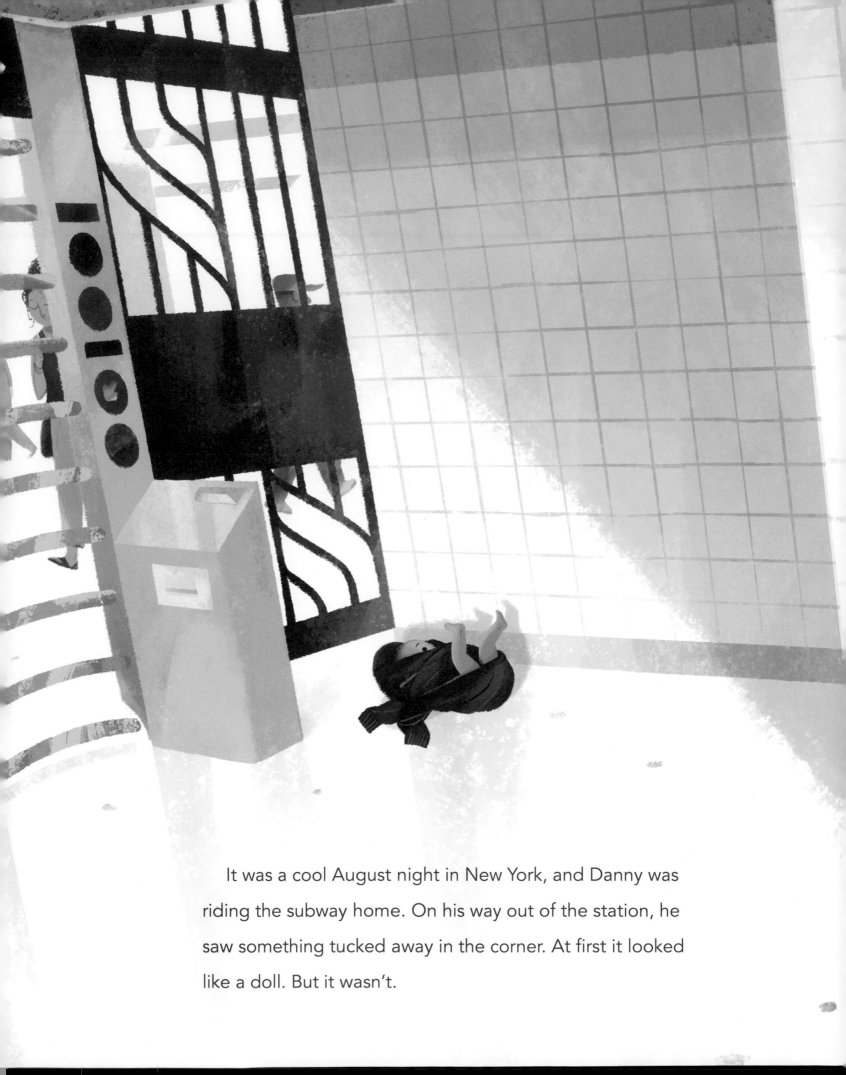

It was a cool August night in New York, and Danny was riding the subway home. On his way out of the station, he saw something tucked away in the corner. At first it looked like a doll. But it wasn't.

It was you.

You were only a few hours old, wrapped up in a sweatshirt. Danny brushed your cheek. You wiggled your arms and legs.

For a moment time stopped. But then Danny jumped to action. He called the police. And then he called me.

"I FOUND A BABY!" he shouted. "Get here quick."

I could practically hear Danny's heart beating through the phone.

So of course I ran.

You were in a police officer's arms the first time I saw you. You looked like an angel, and Danny and I couldn't take our eyes off you. The officer gently put you in the police car, and you yawned as if this sort of thing happened every day. We waved goodbye, hoping we'd see you again someday soon.

A reporter picked up the story, and soon, all of New York City wanted to know more about Danny and the baby from the subway. You made headlines in all the newspapers and on TV.

We didn't know it at the time, but Danny had not just found a baby. He had found our family.

Danny couldn't stop thinking about you, and so the next morning he went to the hospital. But they wouldn't let him see you.

"Only family may visit," said the lady at the front desk.

"I'm the person who found him," Danny said. "He doesn't have a family. I just want to make sure he's okay."

"Thanks to you, he's a healthy little boy," the lady said. "Who knows what would have happened if you hadn't found him? The nurses named him after you and the subway train: Danny ACE Doe."

So Danny and I had to go on with our lives. And even though we had known you for only a few minutes, we missed you. We wondered about you often. We learned that you were placed in a foster home.

Some babies stay in foster care for a short time. Some for a long time. Some live in many different foster homes and grow up without a permanent home or family.

Judge Cooper, the woman in charge of finding loving homes for many New York City children, didn't want that to happen to you. Luckily, she knew how you and Danny had found each other. She had heard about his visit to see you in the hospital. She had seen him talk about you on the TV news. And so she knew exactly where you belonged.

LIVE

NEWS

But first she wanted to meet Danny.

In December, Judge Cooper called Danny to her courtroom.

"You care a lot about this little boy, don't you?" she asked. Danny nodded. "A baby belongs with someone who loves him, and I think that's you. Would you like to adopt him?"

Danny took a deep breath. In that moment, he knew adopting you was exactly what he wanted. "Yes, I am interested, but I know adopting a baby isn't always easy for two dads."

"It can be." The judge smiled. "Where there is love, anything is possible."

Danny was speechless. All he could do was nod again.

He left the courtroom, excited about us starting a family together.

It's funny to think about it now, but I wasn't so sure at first.

"That's incredible," I said to Danny. "But it's impossible."

"Where there is love, anything's possible," Danny said.

"Fate is giving us a son. How can we refuse?"

But I was scared.

After all, our apartment was tiny. Our piggy banks were empty.

I didn't know if we had what it took to be your parents.

A few days later, we went to your foster home to visit you,

and to see if we were ready to be your parents.

Danny cradled you first and then placed you in my arms.

"Your turn," he told me.

As soon as he put you in my arms, you started to cry. I mean, you wailed. Then something strange happened.

"It's okay," I whispered, and brushed your cheek. "You're going to be all right." Suddenly you stopped crying, and just stared at the two of us with these big, wide eyes.

And then you wrapped your tiny little hand around my finger, and you squeezed and squeezed.

The harder you squeezed, the more I forgot my worries. Our home may have been tiny. Our piggy banks empty. But our hearts were full.

That's how we knew we were meant to become a family.

We chose to name you Kevin, in honor of a family member who was very special to us. And our names changed, too. We became your Daddy Danny and Papa Pete.

The miracles didn't stop there, though. We thought we'd have to wait months and months to actually bring you home, but Judge Cooper asked if we'd like to bring you home for Christmas.

For Christmas?

That was in three days!

We didn't have anything for you yet.

But of course we said yes. Where there is love, anything is possible.

All of your new relatives sprang into action to get everything you needed.

Grandma and Grandpa supplied a crib and diapers and footsie pajamas.

Your aunts and uncles

brought bottles and blankets.

Your cousins gave you toys and a teddy.

We stayed up all night reading books about how to take care of you.

Now all we needed was you.

On the day you came home, it was snowing. The flurries floated in the air,

moving in every direction as if performing a special dance just for you.

    We didn't have a car, so we thought about hailing a taxi or hopping on a bus.

But since you had entered our lives at a subway station, we chose to bring you

home the same way.

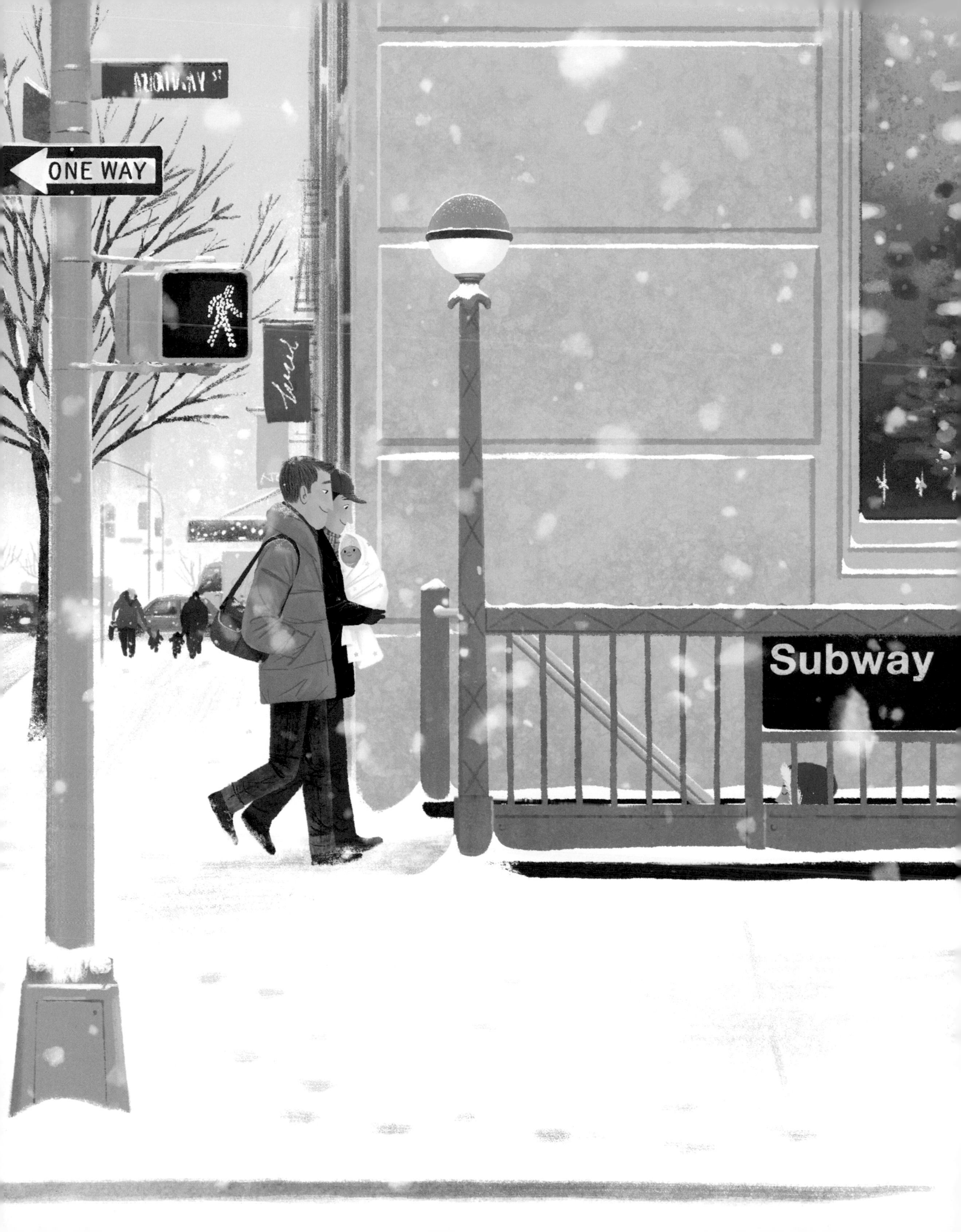
ONE WAY
Subway

We sat in the corner with you on our laps. We were so happy, it was contagious, and other passengers smiled at us.

Soon the rocking and swaying made you sleepy, and I still remember how you looked at us and yawned. Then you closed your eyes and took your first nap as our son.

There we were, the three of us, in a dream we hadn't dreamt but that came true anyway.

Sometimes life hinges on little moments, happy accidents, and
miraculous surprises. Sometimes babies are born into forever families.
Sometimes they are adopted.

And sometimes, all it takes to find your family is a chance glance
at tiny toes wiggling in the corner of a subway station.

Author's Note

The first time Kevin looked up at us with his big eyes, we knew he'd be a curious and observant kid. And sure enough, as he grew, so did his curiosity, especially about how we became a family. In 2012, it was Kevin's idea to ask Judge Cooper* to perform his dads' marriage. So ten years after his adoption was finalized, we were back in family court, this time to get married. Judge Cooper and Kevin were excited to meet each other. They shook hands, until the judge asked for a hug. The woman and the boy who had forever changed and enriched our lives were about to do it again. Danny and I couldn't have asked for a better officiator or best man.

Now in college, Kevin studies mathematics and computer science. He plays Ultimate and is called "Frog" by his teammates for his leaping ability. The boy we once cradled in one arm is now over six feet tall. Kevin has run and finished several half-marathons and full marathons. Together as a family, we enjoy hiking, cycling, kayaking, exploring the national parks, and rooting for the Mets. Judge Cooper has since retired, but we have kept in touch, and she's become a part of our family outside the courtroom.

Pete Mercurio

*Not her real name. She asked that it be changed for privacy.